Struggles Of The Mind

Poetic Conversations To Improve Your Mental Health

CHEVONETTE JAMES-HENRY

STRUGGLES OF THE MIND. Copyright © 2021. Chevonette James-Henry. All Rights Reserved.

Printed in the United States of America.

No portion of this book may be reproduced, stored in a retrieval system, or transmitted in any form or by any means, except for brief quotations in printed reviews, without the prior written permission of DayeLight Publishers or **Chevonette James-Henry**.

ISBN: 978-1-953759-50-4 (paperback)

Scripture quotations marked (NLT) are taken from the Holy Bible, New Living Translation, copyright © 1996, 2004, 2007 by Tyndale House Foundation. Used by permission of Tyndale House Publishers, Inc., Carol Stream, Illinois 60188. All rights reserved.

Endorsements

From the author of Defying the Odds: C.P and Me and Loose to Live, Chevonette James-Henry, comes another riveting book of **inspiration** and **empowerment**.

Struggles of the Mind gives voice to those who battle with mental ill-health. Through its powerful use of poetry, written in the first-person point-of-view, it allows readers to **hear from the hearts** of those who struggle mentally and be able to sympathize and empathize with them. It **removes the stigma** associated with mental illness by providing an **authentic** and **transparent** look into the thought processes and emotions of the embattled mind.

Struggles of the Mind is **transformative** in its ability to take you from victim to victor; from indifference to compassion; from despair to hope, and from merely existing to thriving. Therefore, you are invited to explore and engage with these deep and moving poems for your pleasure.

Kamesha Mellis-Woolcock
High School Teacher, Mother, Youth Worker

It was with great pleasure that I read and appreciate the SERIOUSNESS OF LIFE. This book is already a

BESTSELLER, by its unique presentation of **BREVITY** and getting to the root of everyday struggles. Our MIND is the greatest tool we have to transform our lives from PSYCHOSOMATIC disorders & diseases to a VIBRANT DYNAMIC ENVIRONMENT & PERSON (In simple words, our minds, if not right, can manifest many illnesses).

The author has put the cards on the table: we cannot turn a blind eye from the anxieties, worries, suffering & separation. We are therefore encouraged to lead a HEALTHY LIFE, which will include SPIRITUAL, MENTAL & PHYSICAL well-being. The author has taken a clinical approach, presenting THE PROBLEMS, CAUSES, IN-DEPTH ANALYSIS & ADDRESSING CURRENT WORLD PANDEMIC AFTERMATH & SOLUTIONS: all in POETIC FORM, easy to read & understand. The STRUGGLES are for us all to face: only by education, through the eyes of the educated, like Chevonette, can we make the world a better place. BY GOD'S GRACE, we can overcome these hurdles so that we can safely say: ALL THINGS ARE POSSIBLE!

Dr. Hame Persaud
General Practitioner (Stress Management Educator)

Struggles of the Mind is a MUST READ, and a MUST HAVE for your personal and professional library! It offers the reader a comprehensive, insightful, reflective analysis of mental health disorders. Henry authoritatively and masterfully probes into the dark corridors of this vital issue that plagues and destroys too many lives. Readers will be enlightened and transformed as she takes you on a poetic journey that unravels the hidden struggles, illuminates one's mind, and captivates your spirit.

This book is your bridge that will get you to the other side of wholeness. The author provokes you to identify and embrace your struggles, challenges you to rise up out of them, and empowers you with the will and tools to fight and live the life you were created to.

Ingrid Hunter-Woodstock (Fl, USA)
Gospel Singer, Author, Grade 8 Teacher

Struggles of the Mind is a truly powerful book and an excellent read. The author, Mrs. Chevonette James-Henry, has done the topic justice. The book takes the reader into the intricacies of the struggles of the human mind and provides therapy through the words written therein.
We are told that the Lord Christ, our High Priest, is touched with the feelings of our infirmities (See Hebrews 4:15).
It is very comforting to know that someone else understands our pain and our struggles. The author, through the

therapeutic words of this book, brings that same sense of comfort.

This book will help the afflicted and will liberate them from bondage. Strongholds of the mind will be broken. This book will build compassion and give knowledge to readers who themselves will be used by God to liberate others as well.

I highly recommend this book. May the Lord continue to bless the author.

Apostle Kelly-Ann Brown
Bible Teacher, Children's Department Leader (Ariel Family Church of Love)
Deputy Director of Nursing Services (Bellevue Hospital)

James-Henry's **Struggles of the Mind** is a refreshing and compelling take on a most serious yet taboo issue. It provides a personal, revealing navigation through what can be a minefield of emotions. Hence, it helps us to better emphasize, understand and relate, with these persons, as we all face similar struggles at some point in time. It is encouraging, hopeful, and insightful. This is a life-changing read.

Rev. Brian Doyley

Senior Probation Aftercare Officer

Chevonette "Debbie" James-Henry's **Struggles of the Mind** encapsulates those hidden thoughts, feelings, and emotions we often hide or are told to hide. We are taken on a journey inside the mind rather than bombarded by diagnosis and medical jargons of what could be theoretically correct. We are given a front-row seat in the inner sanctum of the unspoken world of all our minds. It is a book for the sane and the insane, as we all should understand and resonate with the struggles of our minds; that is, if we are not all hallucinating...LOL or maybe just delusional that we don't all have struggles of the mind. Either way, you should read this book. It will deeply move you closer to insanity or faith. On a more serious note, we are real people in a real world with real situations, and we have to be bold enough to be strong enough to know that we are enough to fight through anything we face, and this book can help you through that.

Jody-Marie Beharie
Nurse
Director/Principal (School) - A Gentle Touch of Care Training Institute
Director A Gentle touch of Care Home Health Services

Dedication

I dedicate **Struggles of the Mind** to my cousin, Patrick, who has taught me that despite the struggles we face daily, with the right support system, we can live a "normal" life.

I also dedicate it to every person, be it boy, girl, man, or woman, who faces struggles of the mind daily yet find the will "to be."

Foreword

Mental illnesses affect the way we think, feel and behave. They can be brief or lifelong, in course. Such conditions affect the way we function in school, at work, with our families, friends, and in social settings.

Mental disorders can be particularly profound when they begin early in life. Youngsters with psychological issues struggle to find their own identity and their place in society as they negotiate the demands of academic achievement and social functioning with their peers and families.

This book journals the reflection of teenagers with mental struggles. It highlights, in poetic language, the thoughts of youngsters with mental disorders. This literary work is a voice for anyone dealing with mental health issues. It presents their mental struggles in a reflective and creative way.

As a child and adolescent psychiatrist, I am able to identify with many of the reflections highlighted on these pages because they resonate with the sentiments of so many of my patients. I believe Mrs. James-Henry captured accurately the reflective struggles of the youngsters, who she has been counseling for many years, in her pastoral ministry. As a special education teacher, she is able to understand and fully empathise with them.

There is something in this book for anyone who has struggled with mental health issues. Psychological issues affect most persons at some point in their lives. This book is a must read because it chronicles those thoughts.

Gillian Lowe
Consultant Child and Adolescent Psychiatrist
Senior Lecturer in Child and Adolescent Psychiatry
The University Hospital of the West Indies, Mona,
Kingston, Jamaica.

Acknowledgment

I owe an enormous debt of gratitude to those whose commitment and loyalty to me is unquestionable...my family. My husband, my partner, my best friend, who gives freely of his time to discuss, motivate and encourage, and who is not afraid to push me to clarify titles, explore particular insights, and explain the rationales for the content of poems. Jon-Mark, Jor-Dan and Joi-Ann, my daily doses of inspiration.

I am also immensely grateful to five (5) brave teenagers who spoke to me freely and openly and who were unafraid to show their fragility, and who provided the impetus I needed to write this timely book.

My Editor, Dr. Tesha Thompson, your editorial skills and insights are second to none.

My Inner Circle, who continues to provide much needed encouragement and prayers.

Abba, my Father, whose hand continues to provide direction and whose wisdom I have come to desire above all else. I love you, Daddy!

Table of Contents

Endorsements iii
Dedication ix
Foreword xi
Acknowledgment xiii
Preface 21
Introduction 25
Chapter 1: The Struggle Is Real 27
    Mind Games 28
    Mental Ill-health 30
    Mental War 32
    Mental Garbage 34
    Lost 36
    Homeless 38
    Trapped 40
    Hidden Hurts 42
    Trauma 44
    Battered 46
Chapter 2: Struggles In The Mind 48
    Overwhelmed 49
    Anxiety 51
    Meltdown 53
    Breakdown 54
    Monsters In My Head 56
    Panic 58
    Phobia 60
    Agoraphobia 62
    S.A.D. 64

Social Anxiety Disorder	64
S.A.D.	66
Separation Anxiety Disorder	66
O.C.D.	68
Obsessive Compulsive Disorder	68
Did I?	70
P.T.S.D	72
Post-Traumatic Stress Disorder	72
Insanity	74
Bipolar	76
Dementia	78
Alzheimer's	81
Schizophrenia	84
Hallucination	86

Chapter 3: The Genesis Of My Struggles 88

Domestic Violence	89
Loss	91
Grief	93
Abandonment	95
Change	97
Alcoholism	98
My Unseen Friend	100
Incarceration	102
The Split	105

Chapter 4: Signs Of The Struggles 107

Senseless	108
Sadness	111
Worry	113
Uncertainty	115
Irrational	116
Anger	118
Irritability	120

Frustration 122
Agitation 124
Hostility 126
Antagonism 128
Condemnation 130

Chapter 5: Teen Struggles 132

Bullied 133
Suffering Alone 134
Cuttings 135
Body Marks 137
Raped 139
Cruelty 141
Not Enough 143
Self-Hate 145
Fitting In 148
Silence 150
Rumours 152
Tired 154
Pretension 156
Friendless 158
Litany Of A Teenage Girl 160
Wanting To Be Skinny 162
The Purge 164
Too far 166
Litany Of A Teenage Boy 168
Baby Daddy 170
Substance Abuse 172

Chapter 6: Children Struggle Too 174

Unfair 175
How? 177
Teased 179
Abused 181

Lonely 183

Nightmare 184

The Split 186

Daddy Woes 188

Violated 190

Broken 192

Starved 194

Chapter 7: COVID And The Struggle 196

Fear 197

Isolation 199

Loneliness 201

Emotional Isolation 203

Uncertainty 205

Stress 207

Restrictions 209

Lockdown 211

Unemployment 213

Distance Learning 215

Social Distancing 217

Brokenness 219

House Arrest 221

Chapter 8: Understand My Struggles 223

Stigmatization 224

Humiliation 226

Rejection 227

Condemnation 229

Suffering 231

Toxic Words 233

Labels 235

The Lie 237

Chapter 9: Self-Care And The Struggle 239

Self-Care 240

    Talk It Out 242
    Lean On Us 244
    Keep Active 246
    Eat Well 248
    Will Yourself To Recover 249
    Stay In Touch 251
    Remember Your Voice 253

Chapter 10: Finally 256
    Finally 258
    Be Hopeful 260
    Be Proud 262
    Be A fighter 264
    Be True To You 266
    Be Honest 268
    Victor At Last 270
    Finally, Finally 272

About the Author 273

Preface

"Struggles of The Mind" was birthed by my recent experiences with persons I knew who moved from emotionally healthy, functional, balanced individuals to persons dangling on the edge of emotional ill-health or insanity in a very short time.

Secondly, it was initiated by my recent contacts with five (5) teenagers who had resorted to self-mutilation, starvation, and other self-destructive habits to help them deal with the emotional pains they were struggling with.

"Struggles of the Mind" is therefore designed to call forth a closer look at persons struggling with emotional issues, scars, and pains that threatens to push them over the proverbial edge. It is a call to understand those who suffer from various aspects of mental struggles and to provide a greater understanding and empathy for sufferers, caregivers, families, and communities who are sometimes forced to suffer in silence.

It is designed to provide imagery on aspects of the mind's struggles from a pure layman's point of view.

It brings to you individual poems depicting real-life gut-wrenching and, at times, raw experiences of sufferers of these sometimes debilitating struggles.

It was written with the understanding that the author is not engaged in rendering psychological or other professional services. If expert assistance or counseling is needed, the services of a competent professional should be sought.

Hopefully, **"Struggles of The Mind"** will raise the level of awareness among the general public and initiate the discussion that, in turn, may precipitate major cultural changes, as well as remove the stigmatization associated with any form of emotional instability, mild, moderate or severe.

"Struggles of the Mind" was written with every single audience in mind. Hence, the beneficiaries of **"Struggles of the Mind"** will be all of us – ourselves, our children, our loved ones, the society as a whole who will be encouraged to live emotionally healthier, and longer lives.

Written in a poetic form, you can start the journey from any chapter based on your interests, experiences, and preferences.

It is my desire that **"Struggles of the Mind"** will be widely read. If we are to shatter the silence on emotional struggles, remove the stigma associated with these struggles, avoid the blunders of the past, then we need to change direction, and initiate or continue the dialogue. Now is the right time!

Introduction

Life can get tough. Whether you are a child, a teenager, an adult, a male, or a female, life can throw you a curve ball and crush you to the ground over time or in an instant.

Life is full of hardships, struggles, phobias, addictions, disorders, loss, and death — all of which can leave us feeling anxious, worried, vulnerable, and unable to cope. Surviving then becomes a daily war; a daily struggle.

What do you do when you hit a kilt emotionally, and you are hovering at the brink of a total emotional breakdown?

How can you possibly go on when it feels like your heart is aching with every single beat it takes?

What happens when your emotions get out of control and manifest in your life through negative beliefs, self-destructive behaviors, and actions?

What happens when children and teens see no way out of the struggles they encounter daily and therefore resort to self-destructive behaviours?

What happens when no one seems to understand that every hurt you encounter is a personal one; every scar you bear tells a story?

Struggles of the Mind will take you on an emotional journey as it looks at every day struggles the mind endures, the self-destructive and harmful behaviors that manifest themselves when one feels threatened or excluded, and the different ways the mind deals with everyday emotions, such as fear, confusion, worry...to name a few.

Mind you, **Struggles of the Mind** is in no way insinuating that to be emotionally healthy means the absence of emotional struggles, that life will be easy, or perfect, or there is an absence of unhealthy, negative, or toxic thoughts and behaviours. It does concede the aforementioned but believes in the mind's ability to defy the odds, navigate life's ups and downs with confidence and resilience, and bouncing back when things do not go according to plan or when things go horribly wrong.

"You know when I sit down or stand up; You know my thoughts even when I'm far away." (Psalm 139:2 – NLT).

Chapter 1

The Struggle Is Real

"My own thoughts are sometimes my greatest torment... "

Mind Games

Today, I feel overwhelmingly
empty
emotionless,
tangled in my mind
struggling to explain
to contain
what I myself don't understand.

Unable to smile
unable to cry,
unable to put into words
what's taking place inside,
a contradiction of the highest degree
the pendulum of emotions
overtaking me.

Lines blurred
boundaries unclear
making it hard to see,
to decipher
between a dream
a fantasy
reality.

Except,

my thoughts are racing
at lightning speed
bombarded by
the now, the present, the past,
the horrors of yesterday
the chaos of today
the uncertainty of tomorrow.
Struggling to separate
what's real
from what's not
though they're all merged
in one colossal ball
of confusion.

Mental Ill-health

It doesn't discriminate
It disregards age,
gender
geography
income
social status
race, ethnicity
religion, spirituality
cultural identity.

It affects the way
we think
feel
behave
interact with others
around us.

It determines
how we eat
when we sleep
how we walk
when we talk
what we believe
how we perceive those
around us.

It takes the mind captive
creating instability,
an inability
to think rationally
reason logically,
creating confusion
illusions
an overgrown jungle
of emotional weeds
thorns
thistles
slowly killing
...me.

Mental War

In the middle of my bed, I curled
cocooned like a shell
lost in the myriad of thoughts
flooding my head.

Nothing makes sense
no, not anymore,
So here I am
shielding myself
from the unknown
but from what exactly
I'm protecting
me from?
I don't know
My mind is cluelessly blank.

Tonight, seemed prolonged,
stretched out, never-ending,
Leaving me utterly alone in
my dark abyss
enveloped by stark darkness,
my thoughts and feelings
my only companions.

The shadow of the night

seemed unusually eerie
and quiet,
leaving my mind
to wonder and
wander
about so many things
but about a nothingness
that scares and confuses me.

With nothing to do
with nowhere to go
I eagerly wait
for darkness to fade and sunlight to appear.
Until then, I stare and stare
though nothing really has my attention.
Still, I stare.
Trying to contain my thoughts in this silence
which continues to permeate my space
growing bigger and bigger
getting darker and darker
and with nothing to do
I...stare.

Mental Garbage

Today, I'm drifting from Heaven
to hell
with a ballooned mind
as heavy as lead
descending to a place no one else knows,
where fears abound, and horrors grow.

I'm losing control of my unfiltered mind
besieged by sorrows of every kind
robbing my ability to think
hovering at the very brink
... of insanity.

I seem to have lost total control
of the directions of my heart
and soul
relegated to my secret place
dread and fears overtaking
my space.

There resurfaced all my dormant fears
reducing me to constant tears
negative, toxic thoughts invade
spreading dysfunctionality
to my heart and brain.

So many garbage spilling
from my past
trying to keep up
is quite a task
So, I just let go
Knowing I'd go down and down and down.

From all these emotions, my heart
is reeling
I'm way too tired to fight
these feelings.

Lost

Silenced...
lost
buried beneath the rubble
of the voices in my head
eyes closed,
I'm held prisoner by
memories,
harsh, cruel
overwhelming memories
flooding my heart, soul, and mind.

Pain is now a welcomed anesthetic
for the emotional upheavals
facing me tonight.
Words left unsaid
for a very long time
emotions left unchecked
flooding my heart and mind,
creating an avalanche
of feelings
ignored for way too long
spilling over
invading my dreams
stunning me into silence
yet again

leaving me bereft, alone
...lost.

Homeless

I make my bed here each night
pretending I'm alright
but I'm actually in
a fright.
It will get cold soon
How will I protect myself
from the chills
of the night breeze?

The mosquitoes have
a feast each night.
They smile in glee
as on my naked body
they set sight
Oh, I wish tonight will
be different.
My skin can take the abuse no more
It's a daily battle
living in the
outdoors.

Many believe I'm okay
that my lot is
more than I deserve

No compassion is reserved
for one like me.

Must I die like this?
knowing living is not
fit...for one like me.

Trapped

I feel trapped today
silenced
with nothing to say.
except my mind is like a
run-a-way train
on an uneven railway
bumpy,
unbalanced
endless.

I'm held hostage
by a reality that
doesn't exist
A fabrication
of my daily existence,
none of it
is the
real deal.

I'm trapped in my head
with a heart of lead
heavy with my
own truths
my own version
of life

as I perceive it.

I'm trapped in my own world
my own personal hell
wishing just to dwell
on my pain
my agony
my failures
my self-made misery
which refuses to leave
attaching itself to me
like a second skin
suffocating
the life out of me
leaving me
dead...dead...dead.

Hidden Hurts

Deep, black holes of nothing
that's what you'll find
if you peer deep in my soul
camouflaging
the pains I try so hard to hide
taking out my anger on
those by my side.

I've hidden them well
these wounds in my heart
the feelings that attack me
in the stillness of the dark
when the lights dull and I'm left alone
to mend this heart that has
become a stone.

Hope shattered
dreams broken
plans and desires
all left unspoken
I have nothing left
my life has become quite bereft.

All these feelings have taken a toll
creating an even deeper hole,

but inside me is the worst of all
there's so much chaos, I'm headed for a fall
as vision of happiness fades away,
depression and anxiety seem set to stay.

Trauma

Life has not been gentle.
It has not been kind.
Try as I might
no peace I can find.
I've never forgotten
The day it happened
I lost it all
and great was my fall
from grace.

I still cry in the dark every night,
overcome by the sight
of my recurring nightmare
haunting me everywhere
I turn.

Nowhere is spared
from the flair
of my thoughts
the wanderings of my mind
as it struggles against its own illusion
producing nightmares of varying
degrees and intensity.

Nowhere to hide

nowhere to run
nowhere to seek cover
traumatized by the words that I never said
by the things that I never did
that haunts me that night.

My focus is lost
exhaustion has set in.
Life is static,
nothing moving,
nothing fluid
I feel knocked down,
stuck,
drained,
lacking energy to
rise from the
rubble of the past.

Battered

My body
has become your own personal
canvas
over which you move at will
painting me daily
with your slaps and fists.

The canvas over which
you
roam
explore
and
discover
new territory
new places on my body
to stake your evil claim
as you wound and maim.

Your strokes are anything but
gentle
they're hard
punishing
severe
cruel
they caress the canvas with

unimaginable pains
leaving the marks of your imagination,
transforming every part of me
into a kaleidoscope of wounds
and bruises
most invisible to the naked eye.

Relentlessly
randomly,
daily,
aggressively,
impatiently,
you continue your damage to the canvas
without a second thought.

It pleases you
your power over the canvas
The freedom you've been given
To paint at will
To instill
your mark
As you rigorously pursue
your goal to discover and conquer
as you ravish and capture
every single part of me.

Chapter 2

Struggles In The Mind

"When your mind tells you there is no hope..."

Overwhelmed

My restless days
turns into restless nights.
These thoughts in my head
comes out roaring in the nights.

Days are bad.
I can pretend them away.
But, under the guise of the night,
they seem here to stay.

I'm breaking;
I'm shaking
I'm dwindling away in fear.
I can't seem to contain myself
A breaking is very near.

I have so many flaws;
I don't know where to start
from my messed-up life
To my corroded heart.

My life is just so full
And I'm losing my grip.
I can't take it anymore.

I feel like ending it.

I do not know how to continue living.
My heart is ladened with pain.
I see nothing more for me
nothing else to gain.

So, goodbye
Let me go in peace.
Don't weep too much for me!
I'll be finally at ease.

Anxiety

Butterflies in the stomach
racing heart and mind
feelings out of control,
disconnect between body and soul.

Nightmares
panic attacks
restlessness
trouble concentrating
difficulty sleeping
painful thoughts and memories
all out of control.

Pervasive feelings of fear and worry
faintness
dizziness
shortness of breath
dry mouth
sweating
chills
hot flashes
apprehension and worry
restlessness
distress
fear

numbness
tingling
so hard to handle
so hard to stay connected
to life.

But,
I'm finally learning that
there is nothing wrong with me.
I am not
defective
lazy
melodramatic.
In fact,
I am stronger than this.
I am more than just my anxiety.
I am stronger than my worry.
And, one day I hope to be free of it entirely.
But, until then, I will keep breathing...living.

Meltdown

I'm tired of always lying,
hiding the way I feel,
living life in a bubble,
forgetting what is real.

I no longer know how to laugh.
I no longer care what others see.
Inside this beautiful body,
is a scared and fearful me.

It's hard to pretend you're happy,
when inside you're really sad.
It's becoming harder every day;
not to be perpetually mad.

My mind feels full.
It's difficult to even care.
All these emotions
are creating quite a scare.
My mind needs to relax.
I need to be set free.
This mental overload
is slowly killing me.

Breakdown

It's another one.
I know the symptoms well.
I get all up in my feelings
and my heart begins to swell.

I feel my body shake.
I know a crack-down is near.
For though the time is hot,
my heart is cold with fear.

My throat is dry and achy.
My legs are tingling and weak.
My breath seems ready to leave my body.
I'm struggling to speak.

My body becomes unsteady.
My heart is pounding like a drum.
I'm sure someone is out to get me
and I'm struggling not to run.

I can feel a scream coming.
It's bubbling in my chest.
I'm trying hard to contain it.
But I'm failing at best.

Oh, I feel so hopeless.
I feel ragged and worn.
I'm so tired
of these daily breakdowns.

Monsters In My Head

They scream.
They shriek.
They create havoc in my head
making me wish I was dead.

I want to expose them, but I can't.
Who can I tell?
They all think I'm
crazy
insane
mad
screwed up
psychotic.
So, for now, no one will ever know the truth about them,
my crazy, crazy friends...

They'll never know
how they punish me.
My captors.
My tormentors.
My torturers.

Make me want to do bad,
bad things to myself,
things I can't talk about

because they're too shameful,
too ugly
to admit.

I feel hunted
by hungry, venomous preys.
But I am so afraid of them.
They'll hurt me.
These shadows in my mind.
These twisted, warped reality I am living in
daily.
I'm just afraid
afraid, afraid, afraid.

Panic

One moment I'm sitting still
content
no warning at all that I would be ill.
Then suddenly,
my heart begins
pounding, pounding, pounding.
My head sounding as if bombs are
exploding, exploding, exploding
in my ears
triggering
sweating, sweating, sweating
as water begins
dripping, dripping, dripping.
For sure, I was
dying, dying...dying.

But death would not come
In its stead
dizziness, so merciless
nausea, like no other
clutching my abdominal
in a tightly fisted ball
creating constant worry
that danger was imminent.

A fainting sensation
grave abdominal reaction
fear of dying;
numbness,
tingling
shaking;
difficulty breathing
In a while, I'll experience a reprieve.
Until the cycle starts all over again.

Phobia

They think I'm faking it
but I'm really not.
This irrational feeling
tying me in knots.
It's so persistent.
It will not go away.
Making me scared to live another day.

They think I'm faking it.
But, how could I
envision this perceived threat
which engulfs me, making me want to die?
I want to break free.
But I'm totally unable to.
It's rendering me weak.
Sometimes incapable
of a single coherent thought.

They think I'm faking it.
But they just don't know
this avalanche of emotions
which threatens to overflow
cascading the already fragile
walls of my life
holding me hostage.

Trapped in a lie.

They think I'm faking it.
But if only they could see
this extreme fear which
brings me to my knees
begging for mercy.
If only for a day
before the button on my life
hits replay.

Agoraphobia

You haunt me
like a true shadow.
You stalk me
leaving little hope for tomorrow.
You raped me
taking all my calmness and balance,
all my plans and dreams,
all my hopes of ever being
truly normal.

You enslave me with
your darkness and silence.
You entrap me
with disproportionate fear
heading nowhere, but,
constant worry and despair.
You lied to me
saying there is no way of escape,
there's no clear route to walk
no clear path to take.

Now,
I'm too frightened to break free.
These fears won't leave me.
I'm trapped, drowning deep

in my misery.

My heart is steadily pounding,
as hell seems within reach.
I feel so near to grounding -
with no sign of relief.

I'm fidgeting and bouncing
Sweating, heartbeat racing
with just the thought of leaving
the safety of my home
So, I'll just stay here indefinitely...until.

S.A.D.

Social Anxiety Disorder

I hate being around people.
I see danger everywhere.
I'm klutzy and awkward.
I'm a social nightmare.
Nowhere is spared
a date
a fair
church
all public sphere.

I'm mousy.
Talking to strangers
makes me nervous.
Speaking in public
makes me anxious.
Maintaining eye contact
is nothing less than a chore.
Entering rooms is simple for some.
For me, it requires so much more.
Responding to questions asked
puts me in a fright.
Eating in front of others

is quite a sight.

I'm a wreck,
A social misfit.
I'm awkward,
a social deficit
I'm off-kilter,
an embarrassment.
I'm uncomfortable,
discontent
with who I am.

S.A.D.

Separation Anxiety Disorder

Fear of being away from you
Afraid of what I'll do
if we're ever separated,
I can't sleep.
I am anxious.
Knots are overtaking my stomach.

When you're not here, I get so sad
inconsolable
I miss you so bad.
Life is intolerable.

I can't eat
sleep
I fret
and weep
not wanting to be alone
fearful of what may go wrong
when you're gone.

Nightmare
headaches

stomachache
as I anticipate
the worst
worrying excessively
imagining disaster of every kind
'cause
nothing makes sense
until we're together
again.

O.C.D

Obsessive Compulsive Disorder

Frozen in time.
That's how I feel.
These emotions
are the only things that seem real.
Recurring and irrational
though they may seem,
they keep me safe
in touch with reality.

Obsessions
Compulsions
Fear of contamination
which triggers these
repeated behaviours
fearing any intrusions
from the germs yearning
to get to me.

Checking
Checking
Checking again
The lock on the door.

The spot on the floor.
Fear that germs linger there
or dirt is everywhere
waiting patiently to harm me.

Arranging
Ordering
Things out of place
Pulling
Picking
packing
Washing
the same way, all the time
bringing peace and calm
to my troubled mind.

Did I?

Did I lock the doors?
for the eon time...yes.
Did I mop the floor
especially that spot by the door
that looks sore
to the eyes?

Did I realign my shoes?
My sandals first
then heels
then my boots?
Should I arrange them again?
But, I cannot sleep
until all is perfect
in my head.

Did I wash my hands
before getting in bed?
To be sure, let me wash them again.
I know they're cracked.
I dread the feeling of water again.
But I must do it
or germs will find me
robbing me of my glee.

These repeated rituals
have captivated
yet imprisoned me
I am tired but too scared to fight back
I'm afraid I'll lose control
And lose my fight
to protect me.

P.T.S.D

Post-Traumatic Stress Disorder

Alone is how I feel most days
as I gaze longingly at what was
but no longer is
and will never be again.

Nothing seems sane anymore.
I've lost it all.
My voice.
My vision.
My dream.
My will to live.

My mind is tired.
wired with inner turmoil
pain
anger
depression
emptiness
threatening to boil over
and erupt.

I am a mere shell

hosting a frightened man,
sad all the time
with no escape.
Locked in a vacuum
of
recurrent
unwanted
distressing events
plagued with hopelessness
and these sad
depressing memories.

Insanity

They say I'm
a mental case
a waste
crazy
unhinged
psychotic
mad
disturbed.

Maybe I am.
Maybe I'm not.
Maybe I'm just
a decrepit despot.
Struggling just to be
Me.

They say,
"Smile more,
laugh out loud,
be happy in your skin."
But how can I be any of those things
when I fight so many wars within?

I feel okay now.
The next moment I'm not.

I can hear the voices in my head
fighting for a spot.
But the spots are all taken
by someone else
and they are creating a riot
as they fight for prominence.

I recognize no one.
They're all but strangers to me.
My neighbours, my friends,
even my family.

I know I scare them
but I can't help myself
I have to protect me.
So, I refuse their help.

They all want to hurt me,
to take what is rightfully mine.
I won't give in without a fight.
I don't want their useless words.
They do not understand me.
They've never lived in my world.

Bipolar

I scream
when I'm mean
but that's not the real me.
Stick around and you will see
that surrounding these moods
is a person of immense beauty.

I cuss
when life gets rough.
I growl when I'm out of control.
I'm snappy
when life is crappy.
But I can be real fun when
It's all done.

I don't want you to go.
Though over and over I've
told you so.
I'll soon be okay
Just not today.
I'll soon beg you to stay.
When these cobwebs
go away
cause they muddle up
my brain

causing aches and pain.

Please,
ignore my mood swings
though I know you're wondering
when they will end.
When will I be whole again?

Now my thoughts are racing
and around the room I'm pacing.
There's that tightening in my chest.
I yearn to get some rest.
Now I'm just hanging
suspended between heaven and hell.
This sudden depression
seemed like a lifelong obsession.
I feel euphoric now.
But then, who is this me?
The real me
or my bi-polar self?

Dementia

You looked at me
and I could see
all the questions in your eyes.
Who are you?
Where do you come from?
What do you want?
Your blank stare says it all.
No recognition
in your world that I don't belong.

It's me, I wanted to scream
your baby
The one you held
and fed at the breast
The one you cared for
worked for
The one you gave the very best
of everything you had
Then some.

What do you see, mom, what do you see?
What are you thinking when you look at me?
A stranger, a foe?
Someone from your past?
Someone you knew long ago?

To many, you're nothing special.
Your face reveals your age.
Your body shows some wear and tear,
And your energy is just not the same again.

Too often your memory fails you.
You lose things all the time.
One minute you know what you want to do,
and the next, it may just seem to slip your mind.

But, mommy dear,
please open your eyes, please look at me.
See me, the child you once bounced on your knee.
I do not care that you
have you lost all the time that made up your past;
that all the memories are severed,
and everything seemed lost.

I hope you still hear and can
somehow understand
how much you mean to me.
Though you curse me or forget me,
I'll accept what has to be.
For I will still remember
all the laughter we once shared
How you showed me in so many ways
how very much you cared.

And though it's really difficult
seeing you this way
withering away
I love you endlessly
and will care for you
as we take this journey day by day.

Alzheimer's

I saw you leaving me
saw you slipping away
bit by bit every day
I wanted to beg you to stay
but I was powerless to stop you.

At first, it was the little things
the forgotten skills
the wanderings of the mind
the leaving behind
of the things you had forgotten.

Then it was your inability to dress
to lay down and take a rest
to feed yourself
to take a bath
a task you reveled in
before you struggled to remember the present
as you seem forever locked in the past.

Sometimes I wonder where you're gone.
Now you're only a shell
a mirage
an illusion
a replica of who you used to be

who you once were to me.

You've forgotten who I am
swearing I'm somebody else.
Relegating me to just another face in the crowd
a someone
a no-one
a nobody.

I see you
standing at the mirror conversing with a friend
Not knowing the reflection speaking back is you.
You seem to have forgotten yourself.

Now you sit alone as if I'm nowhere around.
I wonder what is running through your mind,
what memory you've found.
You seem lost in thought
as you stare intently ahead.
You seem trapped inside the prison walls
that was used to house your mind.
The woman that you used to be,
has been slowly left behind.

The body has crumbled.
Grace and vigour long gone.
Still, I hold on
refusing to let you go

though you left me a long time ago.

Schizophrenia

Self-inflicted, they say,
these marks on my skin
but they were put there
by the demons within,
screaming and roaring.
They seek daily to take me out.
They never care.
They're never scared.
They never run away.
They reside here
each and every day.

I want to escape
these demons in my head.
I feel trapped.
like I'm already dead.

Who are these shadows
in my mind I see?
Who are these shadows
who are always watching me?
They look mean.
They look strange.
They look ready to kill.
They just won't leave me alone.

They come and go at will.

Now they're coming to get me.
I cannot escape.
It seems my warrant is sealed
and death is my only fate.

But wait, they're all gone.
Where did they go?
I miss them.
I really do.
But they must never know.
For just a little while,
there's freedom in my mind.
But it was nice
to escape to that
strange world
and leave this one behind.

Hallucination

Please stop these echoes in my head
that tells me I'm better off dead,
screaming on the top of
their voices
scaring me with their
taunting vices.

They make me
nervous
paranoid
frightened to the core
as they rant, screech, and taunt,
invading my battered-worn soul.

Suicidal thoughts I daily endure.
Horrific voices worse than before
The voices escalate,
reducing me to a psychotic state
with a reality I can no longer relate.
Will the voices ever stop?
Will they ever go away?
I'm beginning to believe every word they say.

Distortions, lies, half-truths all seem real.
Darkness, agony, clouds how I feel.

Hateful, spiteful words
they hit so close, they can't be ignored.

They're moving closer and closer
than ever before.
They've all conspired to take
my worthless life
already ladened with
misery and strife.

Maybe I'm better off dead.
Maybe I should listen to the
sounds in my head.
Maybe these voices are really my friends
as they will be with me to the end.
No one can save me right now.
It's done, done, done.

Chapter 3

The Genesis Of My Struggles

"It started and just kept on rolling...a never-ending series of mind-full struggles."

Domestic Violence

I'm surrounded
here,
there,
everywhere.
The kicks
hits
the belts
welts
When will it end?

He's bright, they say
but seem to have no goals in mind.
So, he waste his time
sleeping away
caring not that
learning is taking place
all around him.

They don't know
the chaos in my life,
that I'm re-living the horrors
of last night,
the night before
and the nights before.

If I could just get the
poundings out of my head
then maybe
I could pretend
that I believe
I have a fraction of
the chance they say I have.

But I can't
everywhere I look
I see the fists meeting the skin.
The bruises.
The wounds.
The gashes.
Killing every single one
of my mother's dreams
and mine
So, how can I?

Loss

Shock,
Anger,
Disbelief,
Denial,
Guilt,
profound sadness
has become my perpetual state.
Can't eat.
Can't sleep.
Unable to think straight.
No one can relate.

The pain.
The constant raging pain
has enveloped every inch of me
Leaving me
sated
tired
parched
dry.

"Ignore it," they say.
"It will go away."
"Stop crying now.
Face it day my day."

"It's time to move on.
Time to put it down.
Time to smile.
Get rid of the frown."
"You can't allow it to overtake you.
It will destroy everything you do."
The advice seems fair.
They really do.
But how can I move forward?
Another day without you?
I wish I could just die
and be done with it.
I wish life didn't take you
and left me in a fix.

This anger I feel
is very, very real
robbing my sanity
my ability
to think rationally.
I just can't do it.
I can't, I can't
I can't.

Grief

"Emotionally unstable," he said.
Another name for emotionally dead.
He's not wrong though
that's exactly
where I am
a broken bird
with an unsung song.

I can't help but think of you
I see your face
in everything I do
leaving me
empty
desperate
depressed.

The pain is all I feel
the loneliness is so very real.
Sometimes I reach for you
hoping to hear a word or two
but they never come
and I wonder if I
will ever make it through.

This pathway I've been given

feels unbearable at times
And I don't have the strength
this mountain I can't climb.

I wish this was a dream
and I'm in a
deep, deep sleep.
Then I could regain
my appetite to eat.
Then I could in comfort
lay in my bed
without all the memories
wreaking havoc in my head.
Then life wouldn't seem to be hanging by
a thread
and my heart wouldn't be
emotionally dead.

Abandonment

You were never there
you never cared
I'm baffled.
How could you forget
your own?
What did I do wrong?
What made you just walk away
discarding me like
rubbish
garbage
totally useless.

What was it that I did
or said
that made you not want me?
Leaving me with falling tears,
abandoned, bereft
for so many long, painful years.

Now I'm weary and confused
struggling not to lose
my entire soul,
I have wounds that will never heal,
scars that will never fade.
I've lost all sense of security

all self-identity,
as I struggle to feel
loveable
capable
able
to live above it all
and still be whole.

You left me with my falling tears.
You made me feel like I was no one.
How could you be so cold
to leave me all alone?
Never there to wipe my tears
Never there throughout the years
Never there to hold my hands
when I desperately needed someone
Never there for me to call
Never there to catch my fall.

I don't get it.
How could you?
….how?

Change

I was once the strong one
most likely to succeed
Now I'm just a shadow of
"me"
an epiphany
of unimaginable degree.

All I've achieved
now means nothing to me.
Only a reminder of
who I used to be
how far I've slid
down the ladder
landing in heaps of despair.

I'm drifting
farther and farther away
deeper and deeper
in the mire
of
failure
horror
defeat.

Alcoholism

I grip the bottle very tight
I won't let go until all is right
I'll drink until
my body says no more
then pass out on the
passage floor.

People pass and give me a kick
hoping the action will do the trick
but it never does.
I'm in way too deep
I can't exist without my bottle
except when my body sleeps.

My mind is seldom ever still
haunting memories come and go at will
behind these eyes,
the pain lies inside,
hiding secrets, I wish I could deny

I feel my body shivering
my mind is going insane
The sweat is speeding down my face
falling like torrential rain
but the need still remains

despite the cost, the hurt, and pain.

So I dull it all with a drink
though it makes my whole life stinks
but I don't want to think of all the things I do
the people I hurt while drinking booze
the lives I've ushered into hell
because I can't control
this alcohol-induced self.
So many thoughts rushing through my head
makes me wish that I was dead.

My Unseen Friend

I have an unseen force
who has slowly become my friend
I know you don't believe me
but then
you never do
which is why
my friend slowly replaced you.

I can tell my friend tales
no one else is privy to
It understands my mood swings
in a way you never do.

It dulls the torment of my
broken mind
that has been haunted by
terrors since I was a child.

It takes the sting
from my reality
by providing an escape
from the horrors daily haunting me.

It has become my escape
from the pangs of this life.

If only for the hours
it provides a respite.

You think my friend
is evil personified
but you are so very wrong.
My friend provides the vice I need
to soar above the world
Making me
invincible
indomitable
unbeatable
indestructible
strong.

I know my friend
may soon be the death of me
but for now
it's my only hope of being free
from the demons arresting my soul
plunging me in some deep dark holes
making me cry and cry
just waiting to die.

Incarceration

Behind these prison walls
all is at a standstill
time ceases to exist.
Life as I once knew it
seem to have vanished
like a vapour...smoke.

Time seems suspended
a day feels like a year,
a minute like a month
days and weeks are all the same
merged into one, creating a cycle of
weariness
loneliness
tiredness
fatigue
lethargy
exhaustion.

Behind these prison walls,
the human part of me ceases to exist.
In its stead lies a robotic clone
with hidden emotions.
Emotions?
Those have been ripped from me

torn up,
torn apart.
Piece by piece and limb-by-limb
sanity has left, leaving me with a
never-ending feeling
of despair.

Behind these prison walls
I no longer think for myself.
The system now replaces my voices
my ability to think
my will to choose
my desire to be...anything but crazy.

Behind these prison walls
there's a war going on inside my mind,
depression
has found its voice
its strength
its power
to rule and overrule at will.
Anxiety has taken over my soul,
eating away to the bones
leaving me with
panic attacks so severe, so strong,
a battleground with no end in sight.

Behind these prison walls

There's no hope
just anger
injustice
and a sense of
bareness
a barrenness which scares
and confuses me
A feeling of doom and gloom
an acknowledgment that
life has died.

The Split

My life should have been perfect.
Now I don't quite know what to make of it.
How could it have all gone so wrong
when together we were so strong.

While I laid in bed, I wondered why
my perfect life fell, my dreams just died.
I never planned on you not being there.
Never thought life could be so unfair.
Now I'm left to pick up the pieces,
to pretend my heart is not breaking.

In the days I'm quite alright
but then comes the night
and my life is a fright
in the absence of the light.

I think I'm over the edge
I wish right now I was dead
These thoughts in my mind
are vile, evil, unkind.

I hate whom I've become
fearful
doubtful

isolated
agitated
withdrawn
rarely eating
barely sleepy.
A mere shell.
A wilted flower.
A broken frame.

Chapter 4

Signs Of The Struggles

"They may be hidden, but if you look keenly, you will see..."

Senseless

To you, there's little sense
in the things I do
lying in bed
for days on end
refusing to eat
or to greet
those who came by
to pay their last respect
to offer cheer
to offer love
from above
or just a shoulder to cry on.

Somedays, I just don't care
about the senselessness of my life
the fear
that I may self-destruct
as I sink deeper and deeper in despair.
I just need an ease
from this pain
threatening to sabotage
my fragile, battered heart.

Somedays I feel
I need no one

to move on
I'm emotionally strong.
The conqueror,
the joy I lost.
The cross I bear.
The hurt I feel.
The pain I wear.
In my heart,
On my sleeve.
In my eyes.
Everyday
Everywhere.

Some days my life seems filled with
day to day struggles,
day to day hustles
which goes in vain
goes un-noticed by everyone
by me
by you.

I wish I didn't care
I wish you weren't so entrenched
in my space
in my life
then I could stop the hurt
that perpetuate
my heart

I could then make sense
of these feelings,
this need
to be understood.

Sadness

I'm perched on the edge of a precipice,
a dizzying cliff so high
making the end hazy
and way out of sight.

Today the sky seems invisible
to the naked eye
blocking my view
obscuring my vision
creating a sadness which runs so deep.
It has taken over my soul
cutting my heart
right out of my chest,
as I struggle to believe
that anything is real.

But it's real.
This anger I feel
The pain is
becoming harder to hide
all the feelings I've bottled up
inside,
threatening to erupt
like a volcano spilling hot, potent lava.

I want to run away,
I need somewhere to go.
Around people or not,
I still feel all alone.

I'm sad all the time now.
I realize I'm not
very strong.
Now it's a daily struggle
just to hold on.

I wish I was not so dejected
and crying all the time.
I wish I was getting better
I could even crack a smile.
Then everyone wouldn't
be so concerned
for it's really hard to explain
how I feel
what I feel
without everyone thinking
I'm insane.

No, I'm not insane
I'm just struggling to remain
....sane.

Worry

Every day is war to me,
a struggle to hold on to reality.
Sometimes I just want to die.
I'm so overwhelmed with worry
I just cry and cry and cry.

The constant worrying
is taking a heavy toll
flipping my role
making me negative,
always expecting the worst
restless and jumpy
anticipating a dismal race.

Headaches coupled with stomach-aches
creating tension everywhere,
I'm
trapped in my mind,
with nowhere to go
I'm tired
my heart is slowly breaking down.

Too many questions floating
around my head
weighing me down

making me as heavy as a lead
with no certainties.
My life feels stuck
I'm overcome with the cycle
of my reality.

Uncertainty

I have this nagging feeling
in the pit of my belly
chiseling away my sanity
as I question everything
constantly.

Life's randomness
sweeps away my security
leaving me naked
uncovering my vulnerabilities.
Now plagued with negativity.

I'm fearful of the unknown possibilities
constantly fearing the worst
never expecting the best.
Life has become an uncontrollable test
precariously perched
nothing concrete
ladened with 'ifs.'

Irrational

I don't listen to reason
I don't see the logic.
I defy common sense.
To many, I appear stupid
and dense.

Unpredictable,
sometimes even dangerous,
they say,
a shrew
with a lost screw
no one knows what I'll do
when a situation arises
pushing me to my demise.
My behavior has become
unpredictable
unstable
unreasonable
unthinkable
incoherent
brainless
disconnected
reasonless
flaky
wacky

at the mercy of my emotions
...at the time.

Anger

I hate Him
I hate you
I hate me
We're all doomed
There's no room in my heart
for anything
but hate.

Broken promises
unkept from my youth
lies, lies, lies
never, ever truth.

Broken heart
tearing me apart
my happiness never lasts.
Blocked by the happenings
of the past.

I hate you then
I hate you now
I'll never forgive you
This is my solemn vow.

I hate my life

I want out
It's full of pain
and your both to be blamed.
I will never ever forgive you.
I will not even try.
And as my parents
you will pay for the
years and years I cried.

Irritability

Today I'm happy
tomorrow I'm not.
Today I feel free
tomorrow I'm all tied up in knots.

This minute
mundane things
drive me insane.
Next minute I feel bare
I need my routine
to remain the same.

Now I'm wounded,
tied up in knots
can't help thinking,
of all that I've lost.

My emotions are fragile,
tempers quickly goes awry.
This minute I'm happy
next I'll curl up and cry.

I get more impatient
every single day,
Right now, I'm in the gutters

at least for today.

Angry all the time
anxious all the while
upset easily
agitated daily
frustrated mentally.

Troubled soul, maniac thoughts.
My very shadows scare me,
unwilling to let me be
anything
anything
but me.

Frustration

Never thought life could be so tough
the more I try, the worse it gets,
the sounds of my soul sobbing,
my pillow with my tears wet.

I'm tired and exhausted
I've lost the ability to relax
always clenched
always tense
my mind is always infested
with wasted dream
life bursting at its seams.

Nightmares haunting my sleep
flashbacks
repressed memories
canceled joys
elusive peace
overshadowing my waking life.

I jump at the drop of a hat,
flinch at the slightest sudden unexpected sound.
My existence plagued by anxiety
fear
frustrations of

unimaginable kind
invading every inch
of my heart and mind.

Agitation

I'm nervously excited
stirred up
tense
confused
irritable
pained
stressed.

I'm
antsy
fidgety
happy
sad
mad
glad
aggravated
annoyed
filled with
restless provocation
apprehension.

Somedays many emotions
are happening all at once
irregular, rapid
sometimes violent actions

inner unrest
uneasiness
extreme discomfort
distress
leading to
disruptive behavior
dangerous to myself
and others.

I can't sit still
so I pace and pace and pace.
Can't stay settled,
nor stay in one place.
Now there's an insatiable need
to just
run
and
run
and
run.

Hostility

So intense is my dislike
laced with ill will
threatening to poison
and demonize my soul.

So,
I walk alone
seldom within the company of others.
Some say I'm
distant, detached
unfriendly, unapproachable, unsympathetic,
withdrawn, antisocial....
and maybe I'm all these things.

What many don't see
is that I walk with
head bowed low
shoulders slumped
almost touching the soul
clenched fists
heavy heart
hatred so deep
it's tearing me apart.

Yes,

sometimes I'm verbally lashing out,
behaving in a manner
you consider
threatening
combative
aggressive
evasive.

I must continue to
keep my distance
for fear of being hurt
or fear of hurting...you.

Antagonism

The antagonism between us is so bad
we can't stand the sight of each other.
In one selfish move, you robbed me of my sensitivity
pushing me to insanity.
My feelings for you are ambivalent
at best
deeply hostile at worst.

I don't care if I never
see you again.
Then I would get rid of
all this
bad blood
hostility
antipathy
that has created
enmity between us.

The chasm has gotten
wider and wider
deeper and deeper
separating us into
distant beings
living a lie
inundated

by
half lies
half truths
surrounded by
antagonism.

Condemnation

You assume
it's something I did
in my former life
that made me
like this.

You assume I did wrong
why I'm not mentally strong.
You think I'm weak
because I roam
the street
searching night and day
for reprieve,
for shelter.

You think
that justifies
the stares,
the angry words
the hits
the fists
the labels
the judgments.

I try to hide

how they make me feel
worthless
meaningless
the scum of the earth
fit for nothing
fit for no one
...dirt.
That strips away
my pride
my hard-earned independence
my will
just to be left alone.

Chapter 5

Teen Struggles

"Anything but 'normal' for a teen is like a ticking time bomb..."

Bullied

There is a monster
threatening to destroy my soul.
Its torturing is merciless
consuming me whole.

It's tormenting and crippling,
making it hard for me to cope.
Each day is a living nightmare,
I'm existing without hope.

I'm way too depressed to care.
There's no way of escape
from this never-ending pain,
this unbearable heartache.

This monster is a bully,
his aim is to demean.
Though I kick and scream,
he's destroying all my self-esteem.

I've just given up
I've lost all my will to fight.
My soul is annihilated,
he has taken over my life.

Suffering Alone

I hide it very well,
the constant pain I feel.
In the light of the day,
it almost isn't real.

I play, I laugh,
I do my best to blend in,
but the pain is always lurking
finding a way within.

When the light turns to darkness
and the pain descends,
it's with an all-consuming power
taking my soul
hour by agonizing hour.

You say I'm strong enough.
You say it will get better,
You want me to hold on
and survive this awful weather.

So, I play along.
Hoping every day is a new start
that maybe, just maybe
someone will save my bleeding heart.

Cuttings

It started as an innocent
scratch
just to ease the pain.
Then it progressed
and I did it
over and over
and over again.

Now I do it at will.
I do it to still
these emotions
I can't contain
as I struggle to
remain sane.

I'm hurting myself,
I know,
but the pain will soon go,
unlike the hole
in my part,
the vacuum that's starting
to grow bigger and bigger
going deeper and deeper
sucking me in a mire
a cycle of hurts and pain.

Maybe I'll just bleed out
I'll go without a shout
silently to my grave
finally providing
release...and...peace.

Body Marks

On my arms are marks I made
sometimes with a scissors,
knife or razor blade.
I always keep sharp objects on hand,
for when I need to escape to a friendlier land.

Right now, my body is a total mess
so many emotions, I must confess...
chaotic feelings invading my mind
anger, hatred,
I feel suspended in time.

Intense emotional pain
I endure,
a body badly broken
a bruised, haunted soul.

I exist in a place of no rest
evidenced by the new scars on my chest,
they make me wonder if I'll
ever be
anything but totally free
from the emotions that
have imprisoned me
sentenced to

my own personal
purgatory.

I have lost all my will to fight
so, I exist in darkness
day and night.
Getting through the day
is by sheer survival.
Cuttings are my only escape from
pains arrival.

Raped

I resent him for what he did to me.
I hate him for
violating my privacy,
taking my innocence
raping and degrading me.

I told her
what he did
but she looked at me with
disbelief,
pretending it never happened
because of the spoils
she receives.

Now I'm left alone
to guard this secret of mine,
that those touches never
happened
they're all in my mind.

I wish I could tell
someone
the horrors I endure,
each time darkness came
and he pushed open my door.

I hope someone hears my cry
and listen to what I say,
cause right now I'm
contemplating death
and the thought won't go away.

I just can't take it anymore.
I want someone to understand.
I just don't know what to do anymore.
I'm stuck in my tormentor's land.

I feel imprisoned
with bars inside out.
Help me!
Someone, please!
Hear my silent shout.

Cruelty

You entertained yourself
at my expense
you made me a gimmick just for fun
knowing there's no consequence.
You made me feel weak and small,
you did everything to break me
hoping one day I'd fall.

You are winning
I'm sinking very fast,
I am a loser
the die had been cast,
I was destined to be the bile of the earth
from birth.

I am your punching bag, I know,
but do you have to be so hurtful?
so mean?
so cruel?
so vengeful...so evil?

When will you stop
tormenting me?
When will your conscience
intercede?

When will you see
that you are so wrong?
I'm not very strong
and
you are pushing me to the
edge...of death.

Not Enough

It's hard to digest
what I see in the mirror
each day,
It confirms I'm ugly
just as everyone says.

I would be okay if it lied just a little bit,
if it told me
I'm pretty and just the right fit
but it never did.

I hate this body.
I wish I could change the image of it.
All I see,
is that I'm not thin enough,
not pretty enough,
not tall enough
and definitely not perfect enough.

So, I starve myself each day
though the pain never goes away,
If only I could lose all this weight
and not be filled with so much self-hate,
If only I'd stop being so fat.
If only my tummy would

miraculously become flat.

These emotional scars
will haunt me to my grave.
Each time I think they're gone
then comes a fresh wave.

I'm so sad within
I could end it all with these pills
but...
maybe...not today.

Self-Hate

I look in the mirror
and all I can see
is a sea of insecurities
staring back at me.

There is no beauty
nothing noteworthy,
nothing to cause me glee,
instead, it's a full bag of ugliness
parading in front of me.

My cheeks are gaunt
my eyes are spaced,
my forehead protrudes
as if it's in a race.
My hands are long
my feet are wide,
my smile is so lopsided
I want to run and hide.

My breasts doesn't match
one outweighs the other,
constantly I hide them
from the stares of others.

I wish I had thinner cheeks
longer hair
slimmer body
and ears that doesn't scare,
plumper lips
whiter teeth
nicely shaped belly
not one begging to be seen.

I'm a bag of flesh moving around
with flaws even the blind could see
making me mad
sad
irate
displeased
angry.

I'm fatigued with all these thoughts
in my head
I see no reason to live
I'm better off dead,
I know it seems superficial
and you won't understand
unless you could be me
if only for a day,
then you would see
that there is nothing
absolutely nothing

special about me.

Fitting In

You must be perfect
just to fit in,
can't be too fat
can't be too slim.

Food and drinks, you must never compromise
as you struggle to become just the right size.
Now I'm caught in this coupe
wanting desperately to fit in
with the popular group.

Some say I'm too big
some say I'm too small,
some say I'm too short,
some say I'm way too tall.

Some say I'm a geek
to others, I look like a nerd,
but I don't care
I just want to be
one of the popular girls.

The group seems to like me,
if I follow through with their dare,
but when I'm being myself

no one seems to care.

I've done everything I can
tried everything I know,
but I just don't fit in
and it's really starting to show.

Sometimes I'm really lost and wonder what I should do
I wonder where to go, who to talk to,
life is starting to fizzle and thin,
all because I'm trying so desperately to fit in.

Silence

I am quiet
I'm shy,
in darkness I live
scared, dumb, silent.

You speak to me
I freeze,
my words tangled in the
back of my throat
unable to come out,
fearful of the ridicule that
is sure to come.

Some dare to speak to me
unafraid of those who will
mock them for addressing
the mouse
the one without voice.

Speak up! Some say
turn your head, look my way!
I open my mouth
but nothing ever comes out.

A smack of the lips,

click of the tongue,
air,
yet...nothing.

No one takes the time to learn my name
nor acknowledge my obvious pain.
I'm filled with revulsion and shame
as everyone looks the other way
repulsed by my existence
invalidating my experiences
categorizing me insane.

I'll retreat to my shadows
protected by my silenced
tiptoeing past everyone
noticed by no one
except the nothingness that surrounds me
and let me be.

Rumours

The teasing was harmless at first
then, it became progressively worst.
A half-truth here
A lie there
then the rumors everywhere.

It's hard to believe
lies could spread so fast,
hard to believe I'd
be isolated
by everyone in my class.

Where the rumours started,
I do not know.
Who would do something like this
all for a show?
Who would spread
such sordid, vicious, hurtful lies?
Who would watch in glee
as a teenager's reputation dies?

I feel hurt
isolated and defeated
I'm depressed
heartbroken and discarded,

How will I recover?
I really don't know
So, for now, I'll hide my hurts well
and never let them show.

Tired

Daily I'm pretending
I'm okay.
I don't care
your words mean nothing
of you I'm not afraid.

The truth is, I'm tired
of living my life in fear
of hiding all the scars
from all these nightmares,
tired of the farce
tired of these daily wars.

I'm tired of going to bed crying,
of all the schemes and lyings;
tired of been called dumb.
Tired of feeling mostly numb.
Tired of the hurts... inside.

Tired of being sick.
Tired of watching you humiliating me,
simply to give yourself a kick
at my expense.

You pretend you are innocent

while you perpetuate the cycle of violence
that accompany bullying
just for the fun of it.
It needs to end,
but whose battle will it be?
Them?
You?
Me?

Pretension

These days I find myself lying,
always hiding the way I feel.
I'm lost in a whirlwind of emotions
forgetting what is true or real.

These days I laugh and laugh,
hoping no one sees
the hopelessness on my face,
as I struggle to breathe.

My hands are wet and unsteady.
My heart pounds like a drum,
I have no strength to walk.
I feel stuck in a slum.

Today I don't want to pretend
to be happy
I hope no one asks
why I'm looking so unhappy
lying is becoming quite a task.

My body is engulfed
with shakes that leave me weak,
switching between
heat and cold

I'm struggling to sleep.

I just want to scream.
The world's spinning
upside down
I want to run and hide
I want to sink in the ground.

For now, though
I'll keep pretending
I'm joyful, happy, and free.
My life is simply beautiful
so please just let me be.

Friendless

Friends are important to a
teen's life
but I have no friends
and there goes my plight.

I'm not pretty
I'm not hip
I have no nice clothes
when we venture on our trips.

My hair is not permed
it's rough, not straight
and everything is exasperated
by the struggles with my weight.

What am I to do?
I'm just not cool.
Some say I'm weird
some say I'm a fool.

They all know I'm too shy
I don't have much to say
I prefer to hide in the background
out of everyone's way.

Some say it doesn't matter
things will settle down soon.
I'll soon find someone
to be my friend at school.

But it hasn't happened yet
I'm alone, sad, and stressed.
For nothing has changed
I'm still a social reject.

The forecast doesn't look
too good
though I'm trying to stay afloat
maybe a friendship is
not what life is all about
but,
a friend
my very own friend
would be...kinda nice.

Litany Of A Teenage Girl

I'm a 16-year-old girl
struggling to understand
why in my young life
I'm bombarded with so many pains and hurts.
What did I ever do
to make life so unfair?
Why can't I be
a normal teenage girl?

It's hard to accept,
that there is nothing for me to gain
to see a life
beyond these aches and pain.

I'm struggling through the days
with nonchalance and flair.
No one sees it for what it is
they all decide I'm just weird.

They call me out
they call me names
they whisper insults
ladened with
embarrassment and shame.

My mind is in turmoil
filled with endless struggles
as I try to muddle
through the day
hoping this growing emptiness
will slowly fade away.

But my anxieties are growing
my emotions are fraying
my mind has trouble coping
with the evil meted out
to me.
So maybe,
just maybe
I will end it all
here
and
now.

Wanting To Be Skinny

I starve myself today,
hoping it will pay off tomorrow
for I can't step on the scale
and see anything with a zero
staring back at me.

I'm shedding the pounds
yet it's never enough
I still want to lose more,
and more and more.

I cant seem to stop myself
though I'm living in my own
self-made hell
I don't want to die
so daily I cry
and cry and cry.

Food and I have a strange
relationship
today I love it; tomorrow I hate it
now I'm starting to get real sick.

I'm losing my friends and family really quick.
I must decide if it's worth it

I don't want to lie on a cemetery ground
because I feared gaining a few pounds.

The Purge

Toxic and manipulative,
selfish and aggressive,
that's all they see
when they look at me.

But I'm in a fight
I'm struggling to win,
I'm yearning
for perfection.
I'm striving to be thin.

I love food
So, I eat all I can
then I race to the bathroom
to carry out my secret plan.

All the food in
my belly I expel
leaving my stomach feeling unwell,
like an empty shell.
But I can't let the food stay
in and build
A fatty mound...steely hill.

I know I'm slowly dying each day.

Physically I'm wasting away
but I continue to play my role
as I push toward my goal
of been perfectly thin
I will win...this fight.

Too far

I stuck my finger
down my throat
while trying not to cry
this one feels extremely painful
making me want to die.

Today my body seems
engulfed with stinging pain
as if it's sending me a message
from throwing up to refrain.

I want to listen, I really want to
but my stomach still protrudes
and my shedding pounds are
just a few.

I know it's wrong,
and I'm going way too far
but I cannot escape the feeling that being
skinny is within my grasp.
So on and on I go
trapped in a dangerous game
cause if I stop
my weight remains the same
so, I continue

knowing one day
I'll probably...die.

Litany Of A Teenage Boy

They say I'm a boy
I'm not supposed to cry
I must take life
like a man
by being tough and
Instead of a tear...a sigh.

I can never share my pain
my struggles or my fears
since those emotions
are designated for girls.

I must keep my worries
lock them in my heart
pretend life is good
even when I'm falling apart.

I can never ever show
how I really feel
I can never be myself
I can never be real
For that aint macho
That's not what real men do.

So though so much hurt I feel,

so much anger trapped inside
I cannot let them out
inside they must abide.

This weed is no help
turns out it's a lie
as the problems are still there
after every 'high.'

No one teaches us how to cope
for us, there are no tools
to help us out
Is this what life is all about?
Suffering
alone
...in silence.

Baby Daddy

Thought I was clever
when I started having sex.
Nothing prepared me
for what came next.

These emotions are running
my mind wild.
I wish I had waited
for the appropriate time.

Now I can't eat
I can't sleep.
These feelings run pretty deep,
don't know where to go from here
my mind is overcome with fear.
I'm not ready for this
responsibility
nor this depression overtaking
me.

What will I do?
With whom can I share
this big, big burden
I'm now forced to bear?

School has lost its allure
It's difficult to
concentrate anymore.
My body goes to class
but my mind stays behind
hoping it will find release
at some point in time.

Trapped in a sea of doubts
I feel stuck
with nowhere to run
Nowhere to hide...except locked in my thoughts.

Substance Abuse

They all said it was fun and cool
and not wanting to look like a fool
I succumb,
now I'm numb.
I've become someone I hate
with every fiber of my being.

It's taken over my body, soul, and mind
I now have a master but of a different kind
It's making me clumsy and inept
It directs my every waking step
It tells me how to eat, think and talk
how to sit, stand and walk.

I'm like a puppet on a string
barely coping, just there
dangling.

All it took was just a sniff
when I gave in and tasted it.
Now, I'm a victim without a chance,
my life is gone in just a glance.

I'm realizing this is no game
but too late

I'm destined to a life of misery and shame
cheating, stealing, telling lies
only for a moment, I can feel high.

Now I lay in my bed and cry
praying that I would just die.
Then the hurt would be rid of me
and my soul at peace would be.

Chapter 6

Children Struggle Too

"They think we have no problems...
They are so wrong."

Unfair

He's just a child, they say.
He has no worries,
except to eat, sleep and play.
What could possibly be
wrong with his life
when he knows
no struggles, worries, or strife?

He needs to lighten up.
He's way too serious
for a child.
He needs to find things to do.
He thinks way too much.

Family, counselors,
they all say there's nothing wrong with me
I just need to calm down
stop being so crazy.

They don't know that I'm anxious and worried
I'm spinning out of control
I'm agitated and apprehensive
about things invading my soul.
I have sleepless nights,
internal fights...

if only...
someone would believe me.

How?

How am I to feel
When you curse me every day,
about how I look
how I sleep
how I eat
how I play.

How am I to be normal
when there's nothing normal
about me?
Not my home, not community
not my family.

How am I to be confident
when daily you criticize me
about nothing
about everything
about me just being...me?

How can I be assertive
and strong
when all you see are
the mistakes I make,
the things I do wrong?

How can I be normal?
Tell me.
How do I get there?
How do I move from this
daily life of hate, of fear?

Is there hope for me
really?
Is there any hope
for who I want to be?
Or....

Teased

They call me names
I don't recognize.
They say I'm stupid.
Nothing I do makes
sense in their eyes.

They pick on me
on the playground.
They prod and poke me
when no
adults are around.

They stay far away from me
making me feel really bad.
No one plays with me
making me really, really mad.

Now I'm sad all the time.
I'm tired in my heart and mind.
I don't want to fight them anymore.
I just want to go back to
how things were before.

I hate them all.
I really do.

Yet, I wish they would be
my friends too.

Abused

It's another day in my bed
crying and all alone,
wishing instead of a prison
I was in a normal home.

I'm tired of the beatings,
never being treated well.
My back holds the evidence
of existing in a living hell.

Deep cuts, bruises on my face,
I earned them at her hands.
If she thinks I'm out of place,
it could be a single word
or just a simple phrase.
The beatings and the thrashings
would be administered without grace.

I get no affections.
Beatings are all I got.
My mom is really crazy.
She is a deranged despot.

Home chores not completed,
no dinner for me tonight.

Yet everyone else is laughing
looking happy and cozy
in plain sight.

I must have done something wrong
for her to hate me so.
Since it has been like this
from the 'get -go.'
I can't recall a time it was different
than it is now.
I don't remember ever receiving
anything but daily body blows.

I'm trying to survive
living in this house.
Hoping one day to
escape and see
what real life is about.
No one should live the life I've been
subjected to as a child.
We should play and laugh
and have no reason to cry.
Maybe...one day

Lonely

No one has the time for me.
I'm like a fly in the sky.
No one notices me
among their happy lives.

I'm lost
in my own home
cause though I'm surrounded
by many,
mostly, I am alone.

To be seen and not heard
is the reality for me;
playing games,
watching TV
my daily reality.

I stay out of everyone's way.
I remain in my world.
I entertain myself.
I stay in my bubble
and dream
about that place
where I am free.

Nightmare

I hear the quarreling
as I lay in my bed
trembling with fear
a pillow over my head.

I feel like I'm suffocating
but I have nowhere to turn.
I'm so scared and nervous.
My heart is beginning to burn.

Must they always fight
all through the night?
Must he hit her
with all his power
and might?

How can I help her
when I am so afraid?
When my feet refused to moved
because my body is frozen in fear?

How will this nightmare end?
Is this how I'm destined
to spend
every day

every night
living through this
knowing something is amiss.
Yet not knowing how
to end it all.

The Split

Today they left each other,
my mother and father.
What did I do wrong
that caused them not to get
along?

I can hear her crying
wailing in her bed.
I see the eyes
big, puffy, and red.

I read the questions
flowing from her body.
What went wrong?
What caused this tragedy?

I'm hurting too,
I long to shout.
But I don't want to hurt her more
with the words from my mouth.
So, I keep it all in
and like a recycled bin,
it's hidden away
to resurface
another day

just not...today.

Daddy Woes

I want to meet my daddy
even just once
cause maybe when he finally
sees me he
will give me a chance.

I think about him all day
wondering why he never stayed,
why he had to go
when he knew I would love him so.

Sometimes I pretend
he would suddenly give me a call
or I'd hear his voice
coming through the brick walls.

I daydream
that he'd enjoy playing
around with me.
We would laugh and shout
with absolute joy and glee.

I want my dad.
I want him really bad.
I would give everything.

I would never ever make him mad.

Violated

He touched me.
No one was supposed to know.
"They won't believe you," he said,
over and over in my head
and I believed him.

He had his way,
every single day,
taking my innocence
too early
too violently
not caring that I was only
a child.
He broke my will and took
control of my mind.

The pain right now
is way too much.
Broken,
bruised
torn
relegated to silence
cause no one must ever know.
Oh, how I wish I could get these
horrors out of my mind

and go back to being a child.

Broken

Tired and afraid
I hid in the dark,
hoping tonight
would be the night
you don't want to talk.

Hoping you won't come home drunk,
belligerent
violent
ranting and raging
pouring out your wrath
in words
acidic, volatile words
aimed at me
breaking me down
layer by layer.

Hoping tonight, you won't
blame me for everything
wrong in your life.
All your misery and strife,
telling me how stupid I am,
how you regret having me,
how terrible my future will be,
how I've messed you up

how I'm the cause of all your failures
how I'm the reason she left you
without a backward glance.
I'm the reason she left me too.

There are days I want to love
myself as I am
but I can't.
All I hear are those hurtful words
drowning out my thoughts
my own self-reflection.
All I see are the imperfections
staring back at me.

I want to love myself
but I'm revolted.

Starved

They saw I'm lovable
but that can't be true
cause I've never felt
loved a single day with you.

You gave me clothes.
You bought me toys.
But I've never seen
the twinkle in your eyes
as you look at me
and saw my greatness,
my potentiality.

You feed me well.
They all can tell.
Yet being with you
is like a living hell,
just utter silence
days on end.

No words of commendation,
no praise nor affirmation!
Never 'well done!'
Never 'I'm proud of you, my son.'

I've tried so hard to get
you to care,
win all my races
maintained A+ grades
but they never change a thing.
You simply ignore everything I do.

You are not a bad parent.
You are just way too cold.
Don't know what happened
to your heart and soul,
but I vow to fix it.
I will always try
to hear you say 'I love you'
before one of us should die,
because I love you.
I really do
and I know behind that façade
you really love me too.

Chapter 7

COVID And The Struggle

"It crept upon us
and changed everything."

Fear

I close my eyes to block them out.
All the news that is spread about
and try as I might to slow them down
in my head, they are floating around.

COVID-19 is the new buzzword
crowding my heart with many fears.
It spares no one
and has ripped through lands,
taking many
since it first began.

It's novel, they say.
So, we still don't know
how deadly it is
how far it will go.

It's on a rampage.
No one is spared.
Not rich, not poor.
Not boy, not girl.

It has changed lives.
Overthrown kingdoms,
reset systems and governments

ravaged lands which once seem
prosperous and invincible,
silencing the sick and vulnerable.

It's brought kings to their knees
caring not for their power.
It has its agenda
and won't stop until
many are maimed, many are killed.

So now I'm mostly afraid
because I'm not sure when it
will head my way.
I'm trying to overcome all my fears.
But, they're speeding past my listening ears.

Isolation

How did I get here?
Anxious
irritable
fearful
nervous
longing for company.
If just a sneeze
a wheeze
a sign that life is near.

Day in
day out
cooped up inside
never venturing out.
No sign of my neighbour
behind the wall.
No one to answer
me when I call.
No one to share my fruits with
having no idea what to do with them
when they're ripe and fit
letting them rot...
Sigh.

There's such an eerie silence

permeating every room,
every open space
creating stagnancy
in my body and mind
making me want to scream,
if just to hear my own voice.
I can't take it anymore.
I'm sad all the time
Sigh...

Loneliness

So much to share
but no one to share it with.
So much to give
but no one to give to.
Alone!
I'm all alone.

I haven't had contact
with anyone in days.
I don't even know
if there is an outside anymore.
My peephole serves as
my only contact with the outside
world.

Mornings, afternoon
evenings, nights,
just flows by merging into one.
I have no clue where one ends
and the other begins.

I feel stagnant
going nowhere,
doing nothing.
This isolation

**making me sick
to the core.**

Emotional Isolation

COVID has made me take shelter
inside the confines of this house.
I feel lost
in this place I know so well.
Scared, lonely, waiting for the tide to turn
crying on the inside
slow, silent tears,
pulsating through my entire body
causing pain of unimaginable degree.

I tell myself it will be okay.
I'll live to make it through another day.
But with all these things bottled inside
I feel the urge to run and hide.

Sometimes I just want to sit and cry
without truly understanding why.
I feel so
disconnected
detached
disengaged
cut off
with no hope of it ever
getting better.

The days seemed longer.
The nights lonelier.
Life has suddenly gotten barren.
Everything seems at a standstill.
If only there was another human here
to help shoulder all these fears
to bounce on me a word or two.
You to me, me to you.
Then, I wouldn't feel so all alone
though I'm in my home.

Uncertainty

It crept upon us.
No warning of the devastation it would bring.
The sting it would possess.
Its ability
to bring mother earth to her knees
in panic
frightened
uncertain of the known
fearful of the unknown.

Life suddenly ceased to
be what we knew of it.
The coin suddenly was flipped,
language changed
altered to fit the newness of the time.
Clothing as we knew it
suddenly altered,
making that which was ostracized
accepted.
Our new necessity.

Death seems imminent
with just a stare.
Just an exchange of droplets.
No one is spared.

Now...there is suddenly equality.
All men are at risk:
the rich, the poor
the young, the old
the famous, the unknown.
Everyone a prime candidate
For...death

We don't know what to make of this
new change,
this new way of life,
There's no time to prepare the mind,
to embrace this newness,
this barrenness.
As church closes its doors,
schools are no more.
Suddenly
life has
become unsure.
I don't quite know what to
make of it.

Stress

I see the impact of corona on other neighbouring countries,
and my heart is gripped with fear.
So many questions flood my mind.
So many theories in my ears.

I struggle to equate the damage done
in so little time
knowing it's inevitable that it would
cross this country of mine.

Our safety blanket, as we know it, just seemed
to have vanished in thin air
as we navigate this unknown, novel virus
raging in the atmosphere.

Fear and worry about our own health
and the health of our loved ones,
job losses, layoffs
our financial situations
exasperated by the feeling
that the worst is yet to come.

Loss of the support services we relied on,
changes in work and eating patterns,
difficulty sleeping, slow concentration,

all contributing to worsening of chronic health problems,
creating mental health conditions.

All we see are
exhausted, brave, selfless
frontline workers
risking their lives.
Sick, tormented souls hooked
to ventilators
with no one to hold their hands.
No one to give a hug
as they breathe
their last breath.

And me,
will that be my fate?
I'm apprehensive,
afraid
of what my end could be
if corona beckons me.

Restrictions

No coffee dates
with our mates.
No Sunday family dinners.
No unexpected hugs.
No random conversations with strangers or even
neighbours.

Funerals via video chats.
No way to provide comfort
with a hug or a pat.
So, we all grieve alone
undone by
what we've all become
...loners.

Stripped
naked
vulnerable
everywhere, everyone
a suspect
our loved ones, our friends
our pets.

So many anomalies
from this global pandemic.

So many restructuring
in our workspaces,
shopping malls
families.

So many cants.
So many wants.
So many nos.
So many woes.
So many positions.
So many, many restrictions.

Lockdown

COVID has invaded the nations,
having leaders scrambling to find solutions,
as the virus spirals out of control
destroying economies, lives,
families and homes,
sending us into
total lockdown.

Today, planes are grounded
as traveling is brought to an immediate halt.
Streets stand eerily quiet.
Schools are currently shut and locked.
Bars barren and disturbingly still
as we try to stem this deadly attack.

Friday nights are spent indoors
as parties closed their doors,
sending the music fraternity
in uproar
as it faces the lockdown.

Routines changed.
Work from home the new charge.
Isolation the key.
To avoid a virus at large,

we must all do what we can and more
to survive the lockdown.

Here we are
in complete isolation.
Seniors, immuno-compromised
the most at-risk ones
struggling to stay afloat
as we endure this lockdown.

How long will this last?
We still have no idea.
How will we survive
without losing ourselves
altogether?
When will we stop being a prisoner
in our homes?
When will we be free from this lockdown?

Unemployment

I lost my job today
due to COVID-19, they say.
Hoping that fact
will take away the sting
of losing
my job.

COVID-19 outbreak,
the economic downturn
makes the news no easier to take
when I have mouths
to feed
medication to fill
obligations to meet
bills sitting still
waiting to be paid.

I feel anxious
and uncertain
about today
tomorrow
here, now
the future.

What do I do?

I'm confused.
Where do I go from here?
This is way too much to bear.
How will I cope
when I've suddenly
lost all hope?

I feel precariously perched
on an already unstable ledge
of
needs
poverty
destitution
What's left?
Starvation.

Distance Learning

Nothing prepared us for what
was to come.
When COVID arrived and caused
a lockdown,
distance learning
became a new buzzword
for every parent,
boy and girl.

Students were asked to make the switch
from being physically at school
to learning with a switch.
It was a struggle from the get-go,
to be a student
via the phone
or sit in their room
while learning on Zoom.

But soon children started acting out,
fidgeting
agitating
griping
whining
complaining.
Just merely sitting

with no interacting
was not working
no jesting
no laughing
no playing
no...nothing.

Now it's just too much.
Distance learning seems to have lost its touch.
I'm at a loss at what to do
when this learning finally resumes.
Distance learning has become a real bore.
It's just not easy learning from home.

It feels like life is on pause
with little sign that life will
return to normalcy...
for a long, long time.

Social Distancing

Six feet apart.
That's the new rule
for institutions, churches, market,
schools.
And though staying apart
is no fun.
Preserving life is the ultimatum.

So, we keep our friends and family
in our hearts,
though we are required to stay
physically apart.
We must think rationally.
We must act smart
even though it's tearing
our hearts apart.

Now we're stuck inside
with nothing to do
having contact with only a few,
no hugs
no high fives
no light kisses to the face.
Staying sane during this time
seems like a long-distance race.

For we must stay apart,
observe the indefinite quarantine,
interact with the ones we love
through a computer screen.

The future remains unknown.
It's far safer to just remain home
away from physical interacting
as we continue to practice social distancing.
In the end,
isolation is the key
to remain COVID free.

Brokenness

Doors closed.
Activities paused.
Life has become
intricately poised
by a virus
invisible to the naked eyes.

It's hard to fight an enemy
you cannot see
though it has brought
us all to our knees
begging, pleading for relief.

I had great dreams.
I had great plans.
I had hope for a future
where I could stand
on my own two feet.

Now they're all gone
with the wind
leaving behind
broken hearts, broken things
salvaged dreams
ravaged plans

beyond repair.
Just brokenness everywhere.

House Arrest

Today I'm surviving
not living
not thriving
shackled with an invisible chain
losing a little bit of me each day.

I'm so afraid.
Afraid to breathe.
Afraid to touch.
Afraid to see.
Afraid to live.
Afraid to walk through
my doors.
Life for me is normal
no more.

I needed people.
I need voices.
I need human touch,
physical contact.
I'm craving so much
for the many things I took
for granted.

I'm craving silly jokes

to light up my lonely nights
and sterile days.
I'm thirsting
for people
realizing that people were my drug.
I needed them to distract me from my pain
to keep going when life is like a deluge...
a torrential rain.
Now my world is crashing down.
I can feel my soul dying
a slow eerie death.

Chapter 8

Understand My Struggles

"Mental illness may divide us, but our humanity should pull us together...."

Stigmatization

I hurt myself
not you.
Yet you judge every single thing I do.
The way I talk
or balk
or stalk
or walk
or just be.

You put me
under a microscope
and dissect me bit by bit.
Under the guise that you're trying to
help me,
understand me
but no one does
not him
not me
and not you.

You curse me
denouncing what you see
claiming you don't understand me.
But, have you ever tried
to conceive

my pain?
My world?
My 'warped' mind?
My emotions?
My reactions?
Me?

You institutionalize me.
You say it's to protect me.
But you are really
protecting society
from the scourge,
the dirt,
the mad
Me.

Humiliation

My heart and mind are fighting again,
reeling from the blows
I received from your hands.
When you chose to make me the butt of your childish
pranks
yet again.

Just when I was learning
to blend in,
stay in the dark
to remain invisible even,
you
criticize
and
ostracized me
yet again.

I'm just so tired at this point.
I'm losing hope.
I'm losing my will to go on.
I feel like
just going home
and rest...forever.

Rejection

They say I'm different.
I look different
sound different
talk different
walk different.
So,
daily
they
criticize me
ostracize me
demonize me
isolate me
make me ashamed of who I am.

Now I spend all my nights
screaming from nightmares,
beating myself up,
cutting,
crying,
screaming
wanting to die
afraid to live.
I can't bear the hurt.
I can't stand the pain.
This feeling of rejection

my heart can't contain.

Condemnation

You assume
it's something I did
in my former life
that makes me
like this.

You assume I did wrong
why I'm not mentally strong.
You think I'm weak
because I roamed
the street
searching night and day
for shelter.

You think that my struggles
justifies
the stares
the angry words
the hits
the fists
the labels
the judgments.

I try to hide
how they make me feel

worthless
meaningless
the scum of the earth
fit for nothing
fit for no one
dirt
that strips away
my pride
my hard-earned independence
my will
just to be left alone.

Suffering

I suffer alone
hidden in my dreams
when the light goes out
I struggle to fall asleep.

Nightmares come at will
threatening to still
the beating of my heart
creating newer and deeper scars.

I'm groping around in the darkness
no sun, no stars
no dreams, no goals
just sadness in my heart.

I'm alone, but not by choice.
No one understands me.
No one hears my
silent cries.

I'm always ignored.
It's better that way.
Then, no one has to worry.
They just pretend
my presence away.

Alone is lonely.
But that's okay.
It has become my bedrock,
my refuge,
my mainstay.

So, I'll just continue the way I've been
and not worry about a thing.
I'll just stay in my darkness
at least here
I'm king.

Toxic Words

You wonder why I turned out
this way.
You don't understand what went
wrong you say.
Let me take you down
memory lane.
Let me uncover my years
of aches and pain.

You stripped me day by day
with the derogatory, hurtful words
that made me cry
every single night,
wishing I'd never
see the dawn of light.

You use your words
to enslave me
to believe you were the only one who cared
to chain me to you
out of loyalty and fear.

Those words
still echoes in my brain
as they came like

the deluge of the rain.
You never cared
how they'd made me feel.
You never cared, you were
recreating you...
turning me into a monster.

Labels

The labels I wear are
numerous.
To some,
I'm dangerous,
psychotic
erratic
maniac.

Some are afraid of me.
They say that I will
hurt them,
humiliate them,
stone them,
or
even kill them.

They avoid me
saying I'm
a threat to their children,
afraid I might
maim them,
rape them,
violate them,
mess them up forever.

Could I
really do all those things?
I don't think so.
But then again,
I don't really know.
I can't even vouch
for me...
But somehow,
I don't think...
I would
I could
So, I just stay isolated.
'Me,' my only companion.

The Lie

I had it all. I lost it all.
A man with great pride.
Great was my fall.

I believed the lie,
perpetuated by society
culture
family
that a man is not to cry
not to be real
with his feelings
his longings
his struggling
his failings.

I hid it all.
I pretended to be strong
when all along
I was anything but strong.
I was losing a piece
of me daily.

The pressures of life were too much.
I was overwhelmed,
crying in the dark

seeking solace
for my broken,
fragmented life.

I masqueraded my true feelings,
by being macho,
by 'manning up'
all the time.
When 'manning up' was the
least of all the ways I was feeling.

Now I'm trapped,
with no way of turning back.
My mind is overwhelmed
with the stench of my thoughts.
Everything in me is yelling for help
but no one answers.

Chapter 9

Self-Care And The Struggle

"Taking care of myself is the greatest tribute to me..."

Self-Care

Take some time each day,
just for you.
Rediscover the parts you've lost
to yourself.
Be true.

Start again as many
times as it takes.
Hold your head high.
Live, laugh,
enjoy each moment of your life.

Believe that good things
will happen for you
that you will be great
in all you set out to do.

Exercise, rest,
eat well,
be good to your body.
It will be good to you as well.

Survive,

Thrive,
love yourself,
love others too.
You will need them
in the things you set out to do.

Talk to the people in your life.
Tell them you care.
Tell them you'll need them
when life seems unfair.

Silence your
inner critic.
Time to let it go,
tell it
you're in a better place today
than the day before.

You can do it.
You are wired to win.
Reject the lies your
mind tells you!
Believe the voice within
your heart.
That's always telling you the truth
right from the very start.

Talk It Out

Tell me what's bugging you.
I want to know what you're going through.
Tell me when you're near the ledge
and another argument will
push you over the edge.

Tell me when you're tired and cranky
when you feel pushed
and prodded,
when you feel unhappy.

Tell me when your heart
is full and overflowing,
when nothing makes sense
and you feel like exploding.

Tell me when there's so much in your
heart you want to express,
when you can't contain your sadness
and you're anxious and depressed.

Tell me when you feel nostalgic,
when those childhood memories
flood your mind
making you feel really sick.

Don't decide for me
what you think I can hold
cause I'm here for you
I won't ever, ever fold.

So, tell me
everything
nothing
the whisperings of your heart.
I love you, I'm here for you.
We will never, ever part.

Lean On Us

We don't always understand
the things you say and do;
why today you're cheery and happy,
tomorrow you're evil and blue.

We don't always understand
when you're depressed
and all you do is cry,
when you're ready to give in,
to throw in the towel and die.

We don't always get it
when you tell us you don't care,
when you cling to the past
and sink deeper into despair.

Still, we're here for you
if all you want to do is talk
if all you need is a shoulder
or company when you need a walk.

We'll be there for you,
lean on us
we'll never let you go,
even when you become that person

we do not recognize or know.
Don't push us away
for we are here with you
and we are here to stay.

Keep Active

Get up!
Get dressed!
Laugh loud!
Release the stress!

Get active!
Move around!
Walk a little!
Place your feet on the ground.

Take your muli-vitamins!
Today give your best!
Forget about your hallucinations.
your dizzy spells,
the tightening in your chest.

Take a shower!
Feel the water cascading
down your skin!
Wash the dirt away!
See how clean you feel
within.

Smile a little.
Brighten our lives with

your beautiful smile.
Laugh, chuckle, giggle
despite the horrors
you endured last night.

Breathe.
Take deep breaths.
Let the tension go.
You will be okay.
You must believe so.

Do not give up!
Take my hand, and I will take yours.
We'll get through this together.

Eat Well

Stop skipping meals
because you are not in the mood.
Your body needs the strength,
the fuel from the food.

Food is important
to your daily living.
Eat your fruits and vegetables.
Let them cleanse your
organs within.

Listen to your body
as it pleads to be healthy.
Stay away from substances deemed
harmful to you mentally.

Treat your body as your most
precious tool.
Eat well and sleep well!
A healthy mind and body
are your goal.

Will Yourself To Recover

The journey to health may be
winding and long,
and those that get well are indomitable
and strong.
They fought hard.
Some for months, years,
overcoming pain, depression, addictions,
fears.

They fought the battles that threatened their lives
that caused them so much pain and strife.
They stayed afloat when everything seemed to go wrong
when they were drowning,
they fought to be strong.

They learnt to live above the pain,
holding life tightly above the strain
knowing many have fallen but many have survived.
The goal to recovery, keeping them alive.

We all want you to be happy,
healthy and free.
The very best person you can be:
gentle, caring, honest, and kind
thriving in body, soul, and mind.

**To finally stand above your misery,
motivated by the goal - recovery.**

Stay In Touch

Do not stay away today.
I want to see your face,
and tell you I love you,
I need you in my space.

Get out from behind those walls.
You're pining away,
losing who you are day by day
watching life fleeting by
watching days merge into night
with no respite.

Come sit by me!
Let's have a talk!
Take my hand!
Let us go for a walk!

You use to be talkative,
comedic and fun.
I long to hear your deep laughs
coming from deep down
as you clown around,
wanting us just to laugh
though we'd often pretend your jokes
were as lame as a sad cough.

Come on out!
I'm waiting by the door.
Take my hand and let's explore.
Let's forget about
the worries just for today.
Let's be funny together,
and watch the problems
slip away.

Remember Your Voice

I've always lived in the shadows
preferring to remain obscure,
always relying on the darkness
to keep me hidden
from the prying eyes of those
who'd turn up their noses
at who I am.

No one took the time to learn
my name,
except you.
You who acknowledged my secret pain
while everyone looked the other way,
silencing me with just
a stare
relegating me to my
space and place.

No one took the time
to listen
to the stories I've hidden
beneath the dirt and the grime
as I waited unceremoniously
on my time
to just...fade away

Until you came
and with just one act of grace,
you changed my existence,
acknowledging my right
to be here
listening
to my nothingness.

I surprised myself
didn't know I still had a voice
I've not used it in such a long time.
It sounded unrecognizable to
my own ears.

But it was me, smiling in glee,
laughing and chatting,
forgetting all that
had made me silent for so long,
all that made me believe my
voice had gone with the wind,
disappeared in thin air.

For a couple hours I forgot
about my very own silent world,
and my muted abstinence.
It sure felt nice
to have you listen

to an imbecilic like me,
the scum of society.
Yes, I forgot about everything
except the melodious sound of
my voice.

Chapter 10

Finally

"Give yourself a break.
Stop beating yourself up. You can do it!"

And now, dear brothers and sisters, one final thing. Fix your thoughts on what is true, and honorable, and right, and pure, and lovely, and admirable. Think about things that are excellent and worthy of praise (Philippians 4:8 – NLT).

Finally

Start each day being grateful,
for everything you can.
See the minutest detail,
as a part of God's daily plan.

Live fully,
in every possible way.
Laugh out loud and mean it,
like there is no other day.

Think of something you really like to do.
Get to it, do not put it off,
follow through
even if you're not in the mood.

Following your passions,
be fearless
be bold
pursue
that which is music to your
soul.

Face your doubts and fears,
own up to your worries and your cares.
Stand up strong!

You belong
right here.

Be Hopeful

You will feel down.
You will feel low.
But know
that you're never alone.

You may face harsh downpours
threatening your heart and soul
as you struggle to keep hope alive
hanging on for dear life.
Even in those moments
when you're at your lowest
and life is meanest
be hopeful, you are not alone.

Yes, they're times
life will hurt
and you'll feel crushed in the dirt
but even when you feel there's nobody there
and you're broken by the sheer weight
of what you're experiencing,
be hopeful.
Know you don't stand alone.

And when you feel like
you've lost all hope,

think again.
Ensure that you know
you've always got a place to go,
a solace, and a home.
Continue to be hopeful

because you're never alone.

Be Proud

Left with nothing but
a broken glass
your survival seems to many just by chance
but it is anything but.

I saw you work hard,
harder than most,
picking up yourself
blow after endless blow.

Sticking to the plan
when it must have been
painful to do,
going all the way
always following through.
You've transformed
from a frazzled, worried brain
into a healthy, sober mind again
It's great to see the strides you've made
though you fell time and time and again.

Now look at you
still standing
after being
knocked down

and thrown out.
Living above your limitations
has brought your strength
to the fore
Yes, you've done it!
Be Proud.

Be A fighter

A victim or a fighter?
You choose.
So much to gain.
So much to lose.

A victim justifies, lies
blames, complains,
stores negativity
like juice in a cup,
never fighting back,
finds it easier to just gives up.

A fighter climbs onward, upward
with strength from within,
knowing though struggles come,
you are destined to win.
But you must keep going
each time you're tempted to stop,
knowing you can climb all the way to the top.

Commit to be a fighter
from hereafter.
Believe in your aspirations
and labour.
Strive to be happy!

Strive to live your dream!
Strive...to live.

Be True To You

It is okay to say that you are not okay.
Life is overwhelming!
You are feeling down today.
There is too much to face
when you are having a really bad day.

It's okay to cry
to feel down and out
to want to throw a tantrum
to yell a really loud shout.

It's okay to be true
to say how you really feel
to be vulnerable and naked
without it being a big deal.

It' okay! It really is!
I won't question your truth.
Life is not a quiz.
I know you're human, so you will make mistakes.
But you can overcome your struggles,
whatever it takes.

It's okay if you're not okay
and here's why:

laughing loud is important
and so too the tears you cry.

Be Honest

Be open and honest
with your deepest feelings.
Don't deny that they exist.
Do not pretend all is cheery!
Or the problem will
persist.

Speak out
when others treat you poorly.
It is okay to say that you are hurt.
Stand up for yourself!
Allow no one to
treat you like dirt.

Be quick to admit
your errors.
Apologise
when mistakes you make!
Be fair to yourself and others.
Give as much
as you take.

Be faithful in the little things
you do.
Stand by your words

in spite of what they
may cost you.

Commit to a life
wrapped in integrity,
laced with faithfulness,
lived with sincerity.

Victor At Last

I've seen you
knocked down
beaten up
trampled on
ruled down and out
in a rut
Yet, you're still standing

Chastised
scandalized
ostracized
demoralized
marginalized
and stigmatized.
Yet, you're standing.

Embarrassed
offended
disgraced
defamed
discredited
shamed
humiliated
yet you're still standing.

You've withstood wars
meant to break you,
fights meant to kill you,
situations that should have destroyed you,
thoughts that should have silenced you
and trials which should have imprisoned you.
Yet,
look at you,
still standing
straight and tall
above it all.

Finally, Finally

(Philippians 4:8 - TPT and Proverbs 4:23 NLT)

Keep your thoughts continually fixed
on all that is
authentic and real,
honorable and admirable,
beautiful and respectful,
pure and holy,
merciful and kind.
And
fasten your thoughts
on every glorious work of God
praising him always.
and
Above all else guard your heart,
for it determines the course of your life.

About the Author

Chevonette James-Henry is a poet, teacher, and motivational speaker. She resides in Kingston, Jamaica. She is currently a Special Education teacher at the STEP Centre. She is married to Rev. Dr. Andrew Henry and is mother to Jon-Mark, Jor-Dan, and Joi-Ann. Her passion is to inspire and motivate people to recognize the greatness that lies within them. She is the author of the books: Defying the Odds, CP & Me, Loose to Live, and Loose to Live journal.

www.ingramcontent.com/pod-product-compliance
Lightning Source LLC
Chambersburg PA
CBHW050555170426
43201CB00011B/1701